The Poetry of William Collins

William Collins was born on 25 December 1721 in Chichester, Sussex.

William was educated at Winchester and Magdalen College Oxford and whilst there in 1742 published the Persian Ecologues.

After graduating in 1743 and unable to obtain a fellowship he decided on a literary career.

In 1747 he published his collection of Odes on Several Descriptive and Allegorical Subjects on which his subsequent reputation was to rest. These poems are laced with strong emotive descriptions and a personal relationship to the subject allowed by the ode form.

At the time they gained little notice which was dominated by the Augustan Poets. Depressed by this lack of success he began to sink further into the abyss and this decline was further fuelled by the influence of alcohol. By 1754 he had sunk into insanity and was confined to McDonald's Madhouse in Chelsea. From there he moved to the care of a married elder sister in Chichester until his death on June 12th 1759. He was buried in St Andrew's Church.

Following his death, his poems were issued in a collected edition by John Langhorne (1765) and slowly gained more recognition, although never without criticism.

Now he is very highly regarded and ranked only behind Alexander Pope and Thomas Gray in the pantheon of 18th Century Poets.

His lyrical odes mark a turn away from the Augustan poetry of Pope's generation and towards the Romantic era of Wordsworth, Keats and Shelley which would soon follow.

Index Of Poems
Preface
ORIENTAL ECLOGUES.
Selim; or, The Shepherd's Moral
Hassan; or, The Camel Driver
Abra; Or, The Georgian Sultana
Agib And Secander; or, The Fugitives
ODES.
To Pity
To Fear
To Simplicity
On the Poetical Character
Written in the Beginning of the Year 1746
To Mercy
To Liberty
To a Lady, On the Death of Colonel Ross, Written in May, 1745
To Evening
To Peace
The Manners
The Passions
On the Death of Thomson

On the Popular Superstitions of the Highlands of Scotland
An Epistle, Addressed to Sir Thomas Hanmer, on his Edition of Shakespeare's Works
Dirge in Cymbeline, Sung by Guiderus and Arviragus Over Fidele, Supposed to be Dead
Verses Written on a Paper which Contained a Piece of Bride-cake, Given to the Author by a Lady
To Miss Aurelia C----R, on her Weeping at her Sister's Wedding
Sonnet
Song. The Sentiments Borrowed from Shakespeare
On our Late Taste in Music

An Essay on the Genius and Poems of Collins, by Sir Egerton Brydges, Bart.

PREFACE.

It is with the writings of mankind, in some measure, as with their complexions or their dress; each nation hath a peculiarity in all these, to distinguish it from the rest of the world.

The gravity of the Spaniard, and the levity of the Frenchman, are as evident in all their productions as in their persons themselves; and the style of my countrymen is as naturally strong and nervous, as that of an Arabian or Persian is rich and figurative.

There is an elegancy and wildness of thought which recommends all their compositions; and our geniuses are as much too cold for the entertainment of such sentiments, as our climate is for their fruits and spices. If any of these beauties are to be found in the following Eclogues, I hope my reader will consider them as an argument of their being original. I received them at the hands of a merchant, who had made it his business to enrich himself with the learning, as well as the silks and carpets of the Persians. The little information I could gather concerning their author, was, that his name was Abdallah, and that he was a native of Tauris.

It was in that city that he died of a distemper fatal in those parts, whilst he was engaged in celebrating the victories of his favourite monarch, the great Abbas. As to the Eclogues themselves, they give a very just view of the miseries and inconveniences, as well as the felicities, that attend one of the finest countries in the East.

The time of writing them was probably in the beginning of Sha Sultan Hosseyn's reign, the successor of Sefi or Solyman the Second.

Whatever defects, as, I doubt not, there will be many, fall under the reader's observation, I hope his candour will incline him to make the following reflection:

That the works of Orientals contain many peculiarities, and that, through defect of language, few European translators can do them justice.

ORIENTAL ECLOGUES.

ECLOGUE I.

SELIM; OR, THE SHEPHERD'S MORAL.

SCENE, A valley near Bagdat.

TIME, The morning.

'Ye Persian maids, attend your poet's lays,
And hear how shepherds pass their golden days.
Not all are blest, whom fortune's hand sustains
With wealth in courts, nor all that haunt the plains:
Well may your hearts believe the truths I tell;
'Tis virtue makes the bliss, where'er we dwell.'

Thus Selim sung, by sacred Truth inspired;
Nor praise, but such as Truth bestow'd, desired:
Wise in himself, his meaning songs convey'd
Informing morals to the shepherd maid;
Or taught the swains that surest bliss to find,
What groves nor streams bestow, a virtuous mind.

When sweet and blushing, like a virgin bride,
The radiant morn resumed her orient pride;
When wanton gales along the valleys play,
Breathe on each flower, and bear their sweets away;
By Tigris' wandering waves he sat, and sung
This useful lesson for the fair and young.

'Ye Persian dames,' he said, 'to you belong
Well may they please the morals of my song:
No fairer maids, I trust, than you are found,
Graced with soft arts, the peopled world around!
The morn that lights you, to your loves supplies
Each gentler ray delicious to your eyes:
For you those flowers her fragrant hands bestow;
And yours the love that kings delight to know.
Yet think not these, all beauteous as they are,
The best kind blessings heaven can grant the fair!
Who trust alone in beauty's feeble ray
Boast but the worth Balsora's pearls display:
Drawn from the deep we own their surface bright,
But, dark within, they drink no lustrous light:
Such are the maids, and such the charms they boast,
By sense unaided, or to virtue lost.
Self-flattering sex! your hearts believe in vain
That love shall blind, when once he fires, the swain;
Or hope a lover by your faults to win,
As spots on ermine beautify the skin:
Who seeks secure to rule, be first her care
Each softer virtue that adorns the fair;
Each tender passion man delights to find,

The loved perfections of a female mind!

'Blest were the days when Wisdom held her reign,
And shepherds sought her on the silent plain!
With Truth she wedded in the secret grove,
Immortal Truth, and daughters bless'd their love.
O haste, fair maids! ye Virtues, come away!
Sweet Peace and Plenty lead you on your way!
The balmy shrub, for you shall love our shore,
By Ind excell'd, or Araby, no more.

'Lost to our fields, for so the fates ordain,
The dear deserters shall return again.
Come thou, whose thoughts as limpid springs are clear,
To lead the train, sweet Modesty, appear:
Here make thy court amidst our rural scene,
And shepherd girls shall own thee for their queen:
With thee be Chastity, of all afraid,
Distrusting all, a wise suspicious maid,
But man the most: not more the mountain doe
Holds the swift falcon for her deadly foe.
Cold is her breast, like flowers that drink the dew;
A silken veil conceals her from the view.
No wild desires amidst thy train be known;
But Faith, whose heart is fix'd on one alone:
Desponding Meekness, with her downcast eyes,
And friendly Pity, full of tender sighs;
And Love the last: by these your hearts approve;
These are the virtues that must lead to love.'

Thus sung the swain; and ancient legends say
The maids of Bagdat verified the lay:
Dear to the plains, the Virtues came along,
The shepherds loved, and Selim bless'd his song.

ECLOGUE II.

HASSAN; OR, THE CAMEL DRIVER.

SCENE, The desert.

TIME, Midday.

In silent horror o'er the boundless waste
The driver Hassan with his camels past:
One cruise of water on his back he bore,
And his light scrip contain'd a scanty store;
A fan of painted feathers in his hand,
To guard his shaded face from scorching sand.

The sultry sun had gain'd the middle sky,
And not a tree, and not an herb was nigh;
The beasts with pain their dusty way pursue;
Shrill roar'd the winds, and dreary was the view!
With desperate sorrow wild, the affrighted man
Thrice sigh'd, thrice struck his breast, and thus began:
'Sad was the hour, and luckless was the day,
'When first from Schiraz' walls I bent my way!'

'Ah! little thought I of the blasting wind,
The thirst, or pinching hunger, that I find!
Bethink thee, Hassan, where shall thirst assuage,
When fails this cruise, his unrelenting rage?
Soon shall this scrip its precious load resign;
Then what but tears and hunger shall be thine?

'Ye mute companions of my toils, that bear
In all my griefs a more than equal share!
Here, where no springs in murmurs break away,
Or moss-crown'd fountains mitigate the day,
In vain ye hope the green delights to know,
Which plains more blest, or verdant vales bestow:
Here rocks alone, and tasteless sands, are found,
And faint and sickly winds for ever howl around.
'Sad was the hour, and luckless was the day,
'When first from Schiraz' walls I bent my way!'

'Curst be the gold and silver which persuade
Weak men to follow far fatiguing trade!
The lily peace outshines the silver store,
And life is dearer than the golden ore:
Yet money tempts us o'er the desert brown,
To every distant mart and wealthy town.
Full oft we tempt the land, and oft the sea;
And are we only yet repaid by thee?
Ah! why was ruin so attractive made?
Or why fond man so easily betray'd?
Why heed we not, whilst mad we haste along,
The gentle voice of peace, or pleasure's song?
Or wherefore think the flowery mountain's side,
The fountain's murmurs, and the valley's pride,
Why think we these less pleasing to behold
Than dreary deserts, if they lead to gold?
'Sad was the hour, and luckless was the day,
'When first from Schiraz' walls I bent my way!'

'O cease, my fears! all frantic as I go,
When thought creates unnumber'd scenes of woe,
What if the lion in his rage I meet!
Oft in the dust I view his printed feet:
And, fearful! oft, when day's declining light

Yields her pale empire to the mourner night,
By hunger roused, he scours the groaning plain,
Gaunt wolves and sullen tigers in his train:
Before them Death with shrieks directs their way,
Fills the wild yell, and leads them to their prey.
'Sad was the hour, and luckless was the day,
'When first from Schiraz' walls I bent my way!'

'At that dead hour the silent asp shall creep,
If aught of rest I find, upon my sleep:
Or some swoln serpent twist his scales around,
And wake to anguish with a burning wound.
Thrice happy they, the wise contented poor,
From lust of wealth, and dread of death secure!
They tempt no deserts, and no griefs they find;
Peace rules the day, where reason rules the mind.
'Sad was the hour, and luckless was the day,
'When first from Schiraz' walls I bent my way!'

'O hapless youth! for she thy love hath won,
The tender Zara will be most undone!
Big swell'd my heart, and own'd the powerful maid,
When fast she dropt her tears, as thus she said:
"Farewell the youth whom sighs could not detain;
Whom Zara's breaking heart implored in vain!
Yet, as thou go'st, may every blast arise
Weak and unfelt, as these rejected sighs!
Safe o'er the wild, no perils mayst thou see,
No griefs endure, nor weep, false youth, like me."
O let me safely to the fair return,
Say, with a kiss, she must not, shall not mourn;
O! let me teach my heart to lose its fears,
Recall'd by Wisdom's voice, and Zara's tears.'

He said, and call'd on heaven to bless the day,
When back to Schiraz' walls he bent his way.

ECLOGUE III.

ABRA; OR, THE GEORGIAN SULTANA.

SCENE, A forest.

TIME, The evening.

In Georgia's land, where Tefflis' towers are seen,
In distant view, along the level green,
While evening dews enrich the glittering glade,
And the tall forests cast a longer shade,

What time 'tis sweet o'er fields of rice to stray,
Or scent the breathing maize at setting day;
Amidst the maids of Zagen's peaceful grove,
Emyra sung the pleasing cares of love.

Of Abra first began the tender strain,
Who led her youth with flocks upon the plain.
At morn she came those willing flocks to lead,
Where lilies rear them in the watery mead;
From early dawn the livelong hours she told,
Till late at silent eve she penn'd the fold.
Deep in the grove, beneath the secret shade,
A various wreath of odorous flowers she made:
Gay-motley'd pinks and sweet jonquils she chose,
The violet blue that on the moss-bank grows;
All sweet to sense, the flaunting rose was there;
The finish'd chaplet well adorn'd her hair.

Great Abbas chanced that fated morn to stray,
By love conducted from the chase away;
Among the vocal vales he heard her song,
And sought, the vales and echoing groves among;
At length he found, and woo'd the rural maid;
She knew the monarch, and with fear obey'd.
'Be every youth like royal Abbas moved,
'And every Georgian maid like Abra loved!'

The royal lover bore her from the plain;
Yet still her crook and bleating flock remain:
Oft, as she went, she backward turn'd her view,
And bade that crook and bleating flock adieu.
Fair, happy maid! to other scenes remove,
To richer scenes of golden power and love!
Go leave the simple pipe and shepherd's strain;
With love delight thee, and with Abbas reign!
'Be every youth like royal Abbas moved,
'And every Georgian maid like Abra loved!'

Yet, 'midst the blaze of courts, she fix'd her love
On the cool fountain, or the shady grove;
Still, with the shepherd's innocence, her mind
To the sweet vale, and flowery mead, inclined;
And oft as spring renew'd the plains with flowers,
Breathed his soft gales, and led the fragrant hours,
With sure return she sought the sylvan scene,
The breezy mountains, and the forests green.
Her maids around her moved, a duteous band!
Each bore a crook, all rural, in her hand:
Some simple lay, of flocks and herds, they sung;
With joy the mountain and the forest rung.
'Be every youth like royal Abbas moved,

'And every Georgian maid like Abra loved!'

And oft the royal lover left the care
And thorns of state, attendant on the fair;
Oft to the shades and low-roof'd cots retired,
Or sought the vale where first his heart was fired:
A russet mantle, like a swain, he wore,
And thought of crowns, and busy courts, no more.
'Be every youth like royal Abbas moved,
'And every Georgian maid like Abra loved!'

Blest was the life that royal Abbas led:
Sweet was his love, and innocent his bed.
What if in wealth the noble maid excel?
The simple shepherd girl can love as well.
Let those who rule on Persia's jewel'd throne
Be famed for love, and gentlest love alone;
Or wreathe, like Abbas, full of fair renown,
The lover's myrtle with the warrior's crown.
O happy days! the maids around her say;
O haste, profuse of blessings, haste away!
'Be every youth like royal Abbas moved,
'And every Georgian maid like Abra loved!'

ECLOGUE IV.

AGIB AND SECANDER; OR, THE FUGITIVES.

SCENE, A mountain in Circassia

TIME, Midnight.

In fair Circassia, where, to love inclined,
Each swain was blest, for every maid was kind;
At that still hour, when awful midnight reigns,
And none, but wretches, haunt the twilight plains;
What time the moon had hung her lamp on high,
And past in radiance through the cloudless sky;
Sad, o'er the dews, two brother shepherds fled,
Where wildering fear and desperate sorrow led:
Fast as they press'd their flight, behind them lay
Wide ravaged plains, and valleys stole away:
Along the mountain's bending sides they ran,
Till, faint and weak, Secander thus began.

SECANDER.
O stay thee, Agib, for my feet deny,
No longer friendly to my life, to fly.

Friend of my heart, O turn thee and survey!
Trace our sad flight through all its length of way
And first review that long extended plain,
And yon wide groves, already past with pain!
Yon ragged cliff, whose dangerous path we tried!
And, last, this lofty mountain's weary side!

AGIB.
Weak as thou art, yet, hapless, must thou know
The toils of flight, or some severer woe!
Still, as I haste, the Tartar shouts behind,
And shrieks and sorrows load the saddening wind:
In rage of heart, with ruin in his hand,
He blasts our harvests, and deforms our land.
Yon citron grove, whence first in fear we came,
Droops its fair honors to the conquering flame:
Far fly the swains, like us, in deep despair,
And leave to ruffian bands their fleecy care.

SECANDER.
Unhappy land, whose blessings tempt the sword,
In vain, unheard, thou call'st thy Persian lord!
In vain thou court'st him, helpless, to thine aid,
To shield the shepherd, and protect the maid!
Far off, in thoughtless indolence resign'd,
Soft dreams of love and pleasure soothe his mind:
'Midst fair sultanas lost in idle joy,
No wars alarm him, and no fears annoy.

AGIB.
Yet these green hills, in summer's sultry heat,
Have lent the monarch oft a cool retreat.
Sweet to the sight is Zabran's flowery plain,
And once by maids and shepherds loved in vain!
No more the virgins shall delight to rove
By Sargis' banks, or Irwan's shady grove;
On Tarkie's mountain catch the cooling gale,
Or breathe the sweets of Aly's flowery vale:
Fair scenes! but, ah! no more with peace possest,
With ease alluring, and with plenty blest!
No more the shepherds' whitening tents appear,
Nor the kind products of a bounteous year;
No more the date, with snowy blossoms crown'd!
But ruin spreads her baleful fires around.

SECANDER.
In vain Circassia boasts her spicy groves,
For ever famed for pure and happy loves:
In vain she boasts her fairest of the fair,
Their eyes' blue languish, and their golden hair!
Those eyes in tears their fruitless grief must send;

Those hairs the Tartar's cruel hand shall rend.

AGIB.
Ye Georgian swains, that piteous learn from far
Circassia's ruin, and the waste of war;
Some weightier arms than crooks and staves prepare,
To shield your harvests, and defend your fair:
The Turk and Tartar like designs pursue,
Fix'd to destroy, and steadfast to undo.
Wild as his land, in native deserts bred,
By lust incited, or by malice led,
The villain Arab, as he prowls for prey,
Oft marks with blood and wasting flames the way;
Yet none so cruel as the Tartar foe,
To death inured, and nurst in scenes of woe.

He said; when loud along the vale was heard
A shriller shriek, and nearer fires appear'd:
The affrighted shepherds, through the dews of night,
Wide o'er the moonlight hills renew'd their flight.

ODES

ODE TO PITY.
O thou, the friend of man, assign'd
With balmy hands his wounds to bind,
And charm his frantic woe:
When first Distress, with dagger keen,
Broke forth to waste his destined scene,
His wild unsated foe!

By Pella's bard, a magic name,
By all the griefs his thought could frame,
Receive my humble rite:
Long, Pity, let the nations view
The sky-worn robes of tenderest blue,
And eyes of dewy light!

But wherefore need I wander wide
To old Ilissus' distant side,
Deserted stream, and mute?
Wild Arun too has heard thy strains,
And Echo, 'midst my native plains,
Been soothed by Pity's lute.

There first the wren thy myrtles shed
On gentlest Otway's infant head,
To him thy cell was shown;
And while he sung the female heart,

With youth's soft notes unspoil'd by art,
Thy turtles mix'd their own.

Come, Pity, come, by Fancy's aid,
E'en now my thoughts, relenting maid,
Thy temple's pride design:
Its southern site, its truth complete,
Shall raise a wild enthusiast heat
In all who view the shrine.

There Picture's toils shall well relate
How chance, or hard involving fate,
O'er mortal bliss prevail:
The buskin'd Muse shall near her stand,
And sighing prompt her tender hand,
With each disastrous tale.

There let me oft, retired by day,
In dreams of passion melt away,
Allow'd with thee to dwell:
There waste the mournful lamp of night,
Till, Virgin, thou again delight
To hear a British shell!

ODE TO FEAR.
Thou, to whom the world unknown,
With all its shadowy shapes, is shown;
Who seest, appall'd, the unreal scene,
While Fancy lifts the veil between:
Ah Fear! ah frantic Fear!
I see, I see thee near.
I know thy hurried step, thy haggard eye!
Like thee I start; like thee disorder'd fly.
For, lo, what monsters in thy train appear!
Danger, whose limbs of giant mould
What mortal eye can fix'd behold?
Who stalks his round, an hideous form,
Howling amidst the midnight storm;
Or throws him on the ridgy steep
Of some loose hanging rock to sleep:
And with him thousand phantoms join'd,
Who prompt to deeds accursed the mind:
And those, the fiends, who, near allied,
O'er Nature's wounds, and wrecks, preside;
Whilst Vengeance, in the lurid air,
Lifts her red arm, exposed and bare:
On whom that ravening brood of Fate,
Who lap the blood of sorrow, wait:
Who, Fear, this ghastly train can see,

And look not madly wild, like thee!

EPODE.
In earliest Greece, to thee, with partial choice,
The grief-full Muse addrest her infant tongue;
The maids and matrons, on her awful voice,
Silent and pale, in wild amazement hung.

Yet he, the bard who first invoked thy name,
Disdain'd in Marathon its power to feel:
For not alone he nursed the poet's flame,
But reach'd from Virtue's hand the patriot's steel.

But who is he whom later garlands grace,
Who left a while o'er Hybla's dews to rove,
With trembling eyes thy dreary steps to trace,
Where thou and furies shared the baleful grove?

Wrapt in thy cloudy veil, the incestuous queen
Sigh'd the sad call her son and husband heard,
When once alone it broke the silent scene,
And he the wretch of Thebes no more appear'd.

O Fear, I know thee by my throbbing heart:
Thy withering power inspired each mournful line:
Though gentle Pity claim her mingled part,
Yet all the thunders of the scene are thine!

ANTISTROPHE.
Thou who such weary lengths hast past,
Where wilt thou rest, mad Nymph, at last?
Say, wilt thou shroud in haunted cell,
Where gloomy Rape and Murder dwell?
Or, in some hollow'd seat,
'Gainst which the big waves beat,
Hear drowning seamen's cries, in tempests brought?
Dark power, with shuddering meek submitted thought,
Be mine to read the visions old
Which thy awakening bards have told:
And, lest thou meet my blasted view,
Hold each strange tale devoutly true;
Ne'er be I found, by thee o'erawed,
In that thrice hallow'd eve, abroad,
When ghosts, as cottage maids believe,
Their pebbled beds permitted leave;
And goblins haunt, from fire, or fen,
Or mine, or flood, the walks of men!

O thou, whose spirit most possest
The sacred seat of Shakespeare's breast!
By all that from thy prophet broke,

In thy divine emotions spoke;
Hither again thy fury deal,
Teach me but once like him to feel:
His cypress wreath my meed decree,
And I, O Fear, will dwell with thee!

ODE TO SIMPLICITY.

O thou, by Nature taught
To breathe her genuine thought,
In numbers warmly pure, and sweetly strong;
Who first, on mountains wild,
In Fancy, loveliest child,
Thy babe, or Pleasure's, nursed the powers of song!

Thou, who, with hermit heart,
Disdain'st the wealth of art,
And gauds, and pageant weeds, and trailing pall;
But com'st a decent maid,
In attic robe array'd,
O chaste, unboastful Nymph, to thee I call!

By all the honey'd store
On Hybla's thymy shore;
By all her blooms, and mingled murmurs dear;
By her whose lovelorn woe,
In evening musings slow,
Soothed sweetly sad Electra's poet's ear:

By old Cephisus deep,
Who spread his wavy sweep,
In warbled wanderings, round thy green retreat;
On whose enamel'd side,
When holy Freedom died,
No equal haunt allured thy future feet.

O sister meek of Truth,
To my admiring youth,
Thy sober aid and native charms infuse!
The flowers that sweetest breathe,
Though Beauty cull'd the wreath,
Still ask thy hand to range their order'd hues.

While Rome could none esteem
But virtue's patriot theme,
You lov'd her hills, and led her laureat band:
But staid to sing alone
To one distinguish'd throne;
And turn'd thy face, and fled her alter'd land.

No more, in hall or bower,
The Passions own thy power,
Love, only Love her forceless numbers mean:
For thou hast left her shrine;
Nor olive more, nor vine,
Shall gain thy feet to bless the servile scene.

Though taste, though genius, bless
To some divine excess,
Faints the cold work till thou inspire the whole;
What each, what all supply,
May court, may charm, our eye;
Thou, only thou, canst raise the meeting soul!

Of these let others ask,
To aid some mighty task,
I only seek to find thy temperate vale;
Where oft my reed might sound
To maids and shepherds round,
And all thy sons, O Nature, learn my tale.

ODE ON THE POETICAL CHARACTER.

As once, if, not with light regard,
I read aright that gifted bard,
Him whose school above the rest
His loveliest elfin queen has blest;
One, only one, unrival'd fair,
Might hope the magic girdle wear,
At solemn turney hung on high,
The wish of each love-darting eye;

Lo! to each other nymph, in turn, applied,
As if, in air unseen, some hovering hand,
Some chaste and angel friend to virgin fame,
With whisper'd spell had burst the starting band,
It left unblest her loathed dishonour'd side;
Happier, hopeless Fair, if never
Her baffled hand, with vain endeavour,
Had touch'd that fatal zone to her denied!
Young Fancy thus, to me divinest name,
To whom, prepared and bathed in heaven,
The cest of amplest power is given:
To few the godlike gift assigns,
To gird their blest prophetic loins,
And gaze her visions wild, and feel unmix'd her flame!

The band, as fairy legends say,
Was wove on that creating day,
When He, who call'd with thought to birth

Yon tented sky, this laughing earth,
And dress'd with springs and forests tall,
And pour'd the main engirting all,
Long by the loved enthusiast woo'd,
Himself in some diviner mood,
Retiring, sat with her alone,
And placed her on his sapphire throne;
The whiles, the vaulted shrine around,
Seraphic wires were heard to sound,
Now sublimest triumph swelling,
Now on love and mercy dwelling;
And she, from out the veiling cloud,
Breathed her magic notes aloud:
And thou, thou rich-hair'd youth of morn,
And all thy subject life was born!
The dangerous passions kept aloof,
Far from the sainted growing woof:
But near it sat ecstatic Wonder,
Listening the deep applauding thunder;
And Truth, in sunny vest array'd,
By whose the tarsel's eyes were made;
All the shadowy tribes of mind,
In braided dance, their murmurs join'd,
And all the bright uncounted powers
Who feed on heaven's ambrosial flowers.
Where is the bard whose soul can now
Its high presuming hopes avow?
Where he who thinks, with rapture blind,
This hallow'd work for him design'd?

High on some cliff, to heaven up-piled,
Of rude access, of prospect wild,
Where, tangled round the jealous steep,
Strange shades o'erbrow the valleys deep,
And holy Genii guard the rock,
Its glooms embrown, its springs unlock,
While on Its rich ambitious head,
An Eden, like his own, lies spread:
I view that oak, the fancied glades among,
By which, as Milton lay, his evening ear,
From many a cloud that dropp'd ethereal dew,
Nigh sphered in heaven, its native strains could hear;
On which that ancient trump he reach'd was hung:
Thither oft, his glory greeting,
From Waller's myrtle shades retreating,
With many a vow from Hope's aspiring tongue,
My trembling feet his guiding steps pursue;
In vain. Such bliss to one alone,
Of all the sons of soul, was known;
And Heaven, and Fancy, kindred powers,
Have now o'erturn'd the inspiring bowers;

Or curtain'd close such scene from every future view.

ODE, WRITTEN IN THE BEGINNING OF THE YEAR 1746.

How sleep the brave, who sink to rest,
By all their country's wishes bless'd!
When Spring, with dewy fingers cold,
Returns to deck their hallow'd mould,
She there shall dress a sweeter sod
Than Fancy's feet have ever trod.

By fairy hands their knell is rung;
By forms unseen their dirge is sung;
There Honour comes, a pilgrim-gray,
To bless the turf that wraps their clay;
And Freedom shall awhile repair,
To dwell a weeping hermit there!

ODE TO MERCY.

STROPHE.

O Thou, who sitt'st a smiling bride
By Valour's arm'd and awful side,
Gentlest of sky-born forms, and best adored;
Who oft with songs, divine to hear,
Winn'st from his fatal grasp the spear,
And hidest in wreaths of flowers his bloodless sword!
Thou who, amidst the deathful field,
By godlike chiefs alone beheld,
Oft with thy bosom bare art found,
Pleading for him the youth who sinks to ground:
See, Mercy, see, with pure and loaded hands,
Before thy shrine my country's genius stands,
And decks thy altar still, though pierced with many a wound.

ANTISTROPHE.

When he whom even our joys provoke,
The fiend of nature join'd his yoke,
And rush'd in wrath to make our isle his prey;
Thy form, from out thy sweet abode,
O'ertook him on his blasted road,
And stopp'd his wheels, and look'd his rage away.
I see recoil his sable steeds,
That bore him swift to salvage deeds,
Thy tender melting eyes they own;
O maid, for all thy love to Britain shown,
Where Justice bars her iron tower,
To thee we build a roseate bower;

Thou, thou shalt rule our queen, and share our monarch's throne!

ODE TO LIBERTY.

STROPHE.
Who shall awake the Spartan fife,
And call in solemn sounds to life,
The youths, whose locks divinely spreading,
Like vernal hyacinths in sullen hue,
At once the breath of fear and virtue shedding,
Applauding Freedom loved of old to view?
What new Alcæus, fancy-blest,
Shall sing the sword, in myrtles drest,
At Wisdom's shrine awhile its flame concealing,
(What place so fit to seal a deed renown'd?)
Till she her brightest lightnings round revealing,
It leap'd in glory forth, and dealt her prompted wound!
O goddess, in that feeling hour,
When most its sounds would court thy ears,
Let not my shell's misguided power
E'er draw thy sad, thy mindful tears.
No, Freedom, no, I will not tell
How Rome, before thy weeping face,
With heaviest sound, a giant-statue, fell,
Push'd by a wild and artless race
From off its wide ambitious base,
When Time his northern sons of spoil awoke,
And all the blended work of strength and grace,
With many a rude repeated stroke,
And many a barbarous yell, to thousand fragments broke.

EPODE.
Yet, even where'er the least appear'd,
The admiring world thy hand revered;
Still, 'midst the scatter'd states around,
Some remnants of her strength were found;
They saw, by what escaped the storm,
How wondrous rose her perfect form;
How in the great, the labour'd whole,
Each mighty master pour'd his soul!
For sunny Florence, seat of art,
Beneath her vines preserved a part,
Till they, whom Science loved to name,
(O who could fear it?) quench'd her flame.
And lo, an humbler relic laid
In jealous Pisa's olive shade!
See small Marino joins the theme,
Though least, not last in thy esteem:
Strike, louder strike the ennobling strings

To those, whose merchant sons were kings;
To him, who, deck'd with pearly pride,
In Adria weds his green-hair'd bride;
Hail, port of glory, wealth, and pleasure,
Ne'er let me change this Lydian measure:
Nor e'er her former pride relate,
To sad Liguria's bleeding state.
Ah no! more pleased thy haunts I seek,
On wild Helvetia's mountains bleak:
(Where, when the favour'd of thy choice,
The daring archer heard thy voice;
Forth from his eyrie roused in dread,
The ravening eagle northward fled:)
Or dwell in willow'd meads more near,
With those to whom thy stork is dear:
Those whom the rod of Alva bruised,
Whose crown a British queen refused!
The magic works, thou feel'st the strains,
One holier name alone remains;
The perfect spell shall then avail,
Hail, nymph, adored by Britain, hail!

ANTISTROPHE.
Beyond the measure vast of thought,
The works the wizard time has wrought!
The Gaul, 'tis held of antique story,
Saw Britain link'd to his now adverse strand,
No sea between, nor cliff sublime and hoary,
He pass'd with unwet feet through all our land.
To the blown Baltic then, they say,
The wild waves found another way,
Where Orcas howls, his wolfish mountains rounding;
Till all the banded west at once 'gan rise,
A wide wild storm even nature's self confounding,
Withering her giant sons with strange uncouth surprise.
This pillar'd earth so firm and wide,
By winds and inward labours torn,
In thunders dread was push'd aside,
And down the shouldering billows borne.
And see, like gems, her laughing train,
The little isles on every side,
Mona, once hid from those who search the main,
Where thousand elfin shapes abide,
And Wight who checks the westering tide,
For thee consenting heaven has each bestow'd,
A fair attendant on her sovereign pride:
To thee this blest divorce she owed,
For thou hast made her vales thy loved, thy last abode!

SECOND EPODE.
Then too, 'tis said, an hoary pile,

'Midst the green navel of our isle,
Thy shrine in some religious wood,
O soul-enforcing goddess, stood!
There oft the painted native's feet
Were wont thy form celestial meet:
Though now with hopeless toil we trace
Time's backward rolls, to find its place;
Whether the fiery-tressèd Dane,
Or Roman's self o'erturn'd the fane,
Or in what heaven-left age it fell,
'Twere hard for modern song to tell.
Yet still, if Truth those beams infuse,
Which guide at once, and charm the Muse,
Beyond yon braided clouds that lie,
Paving the light embroider'd sky,
Amidst the bright pavilion'd plains,
The beauteous model still remains.
There, happier than in islands blest,
Or bowers by spring or Hebe drest,
The chiefs who fill our Albion's story,
In warlike weeds, retired in glory,
Hear their consorted Druids sing
Their triumphs to the immortal string.
How may the poet now unfold
What never tongue or numbers told?
How learn delighted, and amazed,
What hands unknown that fabric raised?
Even now before his favour'd eyes,
In gothic pride, it seems to rise!
Yet Græcia's graceful orders join,
Majestic through the mix'd design:
The secret builder knew to choose
Each sphere-found gem of richest hues;
Whate'er heaven's purer mould contains,
When nearer suns emblaze its veins;
There on the walls the patriot's sight
May ever hang with fresh delight,
And, graved with some prophetic rage,
Read Albion's fame through every age.
Ye forms divine, ye laureat band,
That near her inmost altar stand!
Now soothe her to her blissful train
Blithe Concord's social form to gain;
Concord, whose myrtle wand can steep
Even Anger's bloodshot eyes in sleep;
Before whose breathing bosom's balm
Rage drops his steel, and storms grow calm:
Her let our sires and matrons hoar
Welcome to Briton's ravaged shore;
Our youths, enamour'd of the fair,
Play with the tangles of her hair,

Till, in one loud applauding sound,
The nations shout to her around,
O how supremely art thou blest,
Thou, lady, thou shalt rule the west!

ODE TO A LADY, ON THE DEATH OF COLONEL ROSS, IN THE ACTION OF FONTENOY.

Written in May, 1745.

While, lost to all his former mirth,
Britannia's genius bends to earth,
And mourns the fatal day:
While stain'd with blood he strives to tear
Unseemly from his sea-green hair
The wreaths of cheerful May:

The thoughts which musing Pity pays,
And fond Remembrance loves to raise,
Your faithful hours attend;
Still Fancy, to herself unkind,
Awakes to grief the soften'd mind,
And points the bleeding friend.

By rapid Scheld's descending wave
His country's vows shall bless the grave,
Where'er the youth is laid:
That sacred spot the village hind
With every sweetest turf shall bind,
And Peace protect the shade.

Blest youth, regardful of thy doom,
Aërial hands shall build thy tomb,
With shadowy trophies crown'd;
Whilst Honour bathed in tears shall rove
To sigh thy name through every grove,
And call his heroes round.

The warlike dead of every age,
Who fill the fair recording page,
Shall leave their sainted rest;
And, half reclining on his spear,
Each wondering chief by turns appear,
To hail the blooming guest:

Old Edward's sons, unknown to yield,
Shall crowd from Cressy's laurel'd field,
And gaze with fix'd delight;
Again for Britain's wrongs they feel,
Again they snatch the gleamy steel,

And wish the avenging fight.

But lo, where, sunk in deep despair,
Her garments torn, her bosom bare,
Impatient Freedom lies!
Her matted tresses madly spread,
To every sod, which wraps the dead,
She turns her joyless eyes.

Ne'er shall she leave that lowly ground
Till notes of triumph bursting round
Proclaim her reign restored:
Till William seek the sad retreat,
And, bleeding at her sacred feet,
Present the sated sword.

If, weak to soothe so soft a heart,
These pictured glories nought impart,
To dry thy constant tear:
If, yet, in Sorrow's distant eye,
Exposed and pale thou see'st him lie,
Wild War insulting near:

Where'er from time thou court'st relief,
The Muse shall still, with social grief,
Her gentlest promise keep;
Even humbled Harting's cottaged vale
Shall learn the sad repeated tale,
And bid her shepherds weep.

ODE TO EVENING.

If aught of oaten stop, or pastoral song,
May hope, chaste Eve, to soothe thy modest ear,
Like thy own brawling springs,
Thy springs, and dying gales;

O Nymph reserved, while now the bright-hair'd sun
Sits in yon western tent, whose cloudy skirts,
With brede ethereal wove,
O'erhang his wavy bed:

Now air is hush'd, save where the weak-eyed bat
With short shrill shriek flits by on leathern wing;
Or where the beetle winds
His small but sullen horn,

As oft he rises 'midst the twilight path,
Against the pilgrim borne in heedless hum:
Now teach me, maid composed,

To breathe some soften'd strain,

Whose numbers, stealing through thy darkening vale,
May not unseemly with its stillness suit;
As, musing slow, I hail
Thy genial loved return!

For when thy folding-star arising shows
His paly circlet, at his warning lamp
The fragrant Hours, and Elves
Who slept in buds the day,

And many a Nymph who wreathes her brows with sedge,
And sheds the freshening dew, and, lovelier still,
The pensive Pleasures sweet,
Prepare thy shadowy car.

Then let me rove some wild and heathy scene;
Or find some ruin, 'midst its dreary dells,
Whose walls more awful nod
By thy religious gleams.

Or, if chill blustering winds, or driving rain,
Prevent my willing feet, be mine the hut,
That, from the mountain's side,
Views wilds, and swelling floods,

And hamlets brown, and dim-discover'd spires;
And hears their simple bell, and marks o'er all
Thy dewy fingers draw
The gradual dusky veil.

While Spring shall pour his showers, as oft he wont,
And bathe thy breathing tresses, meekest Eve!
While Summer loves to sport
Beneath thy lingering light;

While sallow Autumn fills thy lap with leaves;
Or Winter, yelling through the troublous air,
Affrights thy shrinking train,
And rudely rends thy robes;

So long, regardful of thy quiet rule,
Shall Fancy, Friendship, Science, smiling Peace,
Thy gentlest influence own,
And love thy favourite name!

ODE TO PEACE.
O thou, who bad'st thy turtles bear

Swift from his grasp thy golden hair,
And sought'st thy native skies;
When War, by vultures drawn from far,
To Britain bent his iron car,
And bade his storms arise!

Tired of his rude tyrannic sway,
Our youth shall fix some festive day,
His sullen shrines to burn:
But thou who hear'st the turning spheres,
What sounds may charm thy partial ears,
And gain thy blest return!

O Peace, thy injured robes up-bind!
O rise! and leave not one behind
Of all thy beamy train;
The British Lion, goddess sweet,
Lies stretch'd on earth to kiss thy feet,
And own thy holier reign.

Let others court thy transient smile,
But come to grace thy western isle,
By warlike Honour led;
And, while around her ports rejoice,
While all her sons adore thy choice,
With him forever wed!

THE MANNERS. AN ODE.
Farewell, for clearer ken design'd,
The dim-discover'd tracts of mind;
Truths which, from action's paths retired,
My silent search in vain required!
No more my sail that deep explores;
No more I search those magic shores;
What regions part the world of soul,
Or whence thy streams, Opinion, roll:
If e'er I round such fairy field,
Some power impart the spear and shield,
At which the wizard Passions fly;
By which the giant Follies die!

Farewell the porch whose roof is seen
Arch'd with the enlivening olive's green:
Where Science, prank'd in tissued vest,
By Reason, Pride, and Fancy drest,
Comes, like a bride, so trim array'd,
To wed with Doubt in Plato's shade!

Youth of the quick uncheated sight,

Thy walks, Observance, more invite!
O thou who lovest that ampler range,
Where life's wide prospects round thee change,
And, with her mingling sons allied,
Throw'st the prattling page aside,
To me, in converse sweet, impart
To read in man the native heart;
To learn, where Science sure is found,
From Nature as she lives around;
And, gazing oft her mirror true,
By turns each shifting image view!
Till meddling Art's officious lore
Reverse the lessons taught before;
Alluring from a safer rule,
To dream in her enchanted school:
Thou, Heaven, whate'er of great we boast,
Hast blest this social science most.

Retiring hence to thoughtful cell,
As Fancy breathes her potent spell,
Not vain she finds the charmful task,
In pageant quaint, in motley mask;
Behold, before her musing eyes,
The countless Manners round her rise;
While, ever varying as they pass,
To some Contempt applies her glass:
With these the white-robed maids combine;
And those the laughing satyrs join!
But who is he whom now she views,
In robe of wild contending hues?
Thou by the Passions nursed, I greet
The comic sock that binds thy feet!
O Humour, thou whose name is known
To Britain's favour'd isle alone:
Me too amidst thy band admit;
There where the young-eyed healthful Wit,
(Whose jewels in his crispéd hair
Are placed each other's beams to share;
Whom no delights from thee divide)
In laughter loosed, attends thy side.

By old Miletus, who so long
Has ceased his love-inwoven song;
By all you taught the Tuscan maids,
In changed Italia's modern shades;
By him whose knight's distinguish'd name
Refined a nation's lust of fame;
Whose tales e'en now, with echoes sweet,
Castilia's Moorish hills repeat;
Or him whom Seine's blue nymphs deplore,
In watchet weeds on Gallia's shore;

Who drew the sad Sicilian maid,
By virtues in her sire betray'd.

O Nature boon, from whom proceed
Each forceful thought, each prompted deed;
If but from thee I hope to feel,
On all my heart imprint thy seal!
Let some retreating cynic find
Those oft-turn'd scrolls I leave behind:
The Sports and I this hour agree,
To rove thy scene-full world with thee!

THE PASSIONS. AN ODE FOR MUSIC.
Performed at Oxford, with Hayes's music, in 1750.

When Music, heavenly maid, was young,
While yet in early Greece she sung,
The Passions oft, to hear her shell,
Throng'd around her magic cell,
Exulting, trembling, raging, fainting,
Possest beyond the Muse's painting:
By turns they felt the glowing mind
Disturb'd, delighted, raised, refined;
Till once, 'tis said, when all were fired,
Fill'd with fury, rapt, inspired,
From the supporting myrtles round
They snatch'd her instruments of sound;
And, as they oft had heard apart
Sweet lessons of her forceful art,
Each (for Madness ruled the hour)
Would prove his own expressive power.

First Fear his hand, its skill to try,
Amid the chords bewilder'd laid,
And back recoil'd, he knew not why,
E'en at the sound himself had made.

Next Anger rush'd; his eyes on fire,
In lightnings own'd his secret stings:
In one rude clash he struck the lyre,
And swept with hurried hand the strings.

With woful measures wan Despair
Low, sullen sounds his grief beguiled;
A solemn, strange, and mingled air;
'Twas sad by fits, by starts 'twas wild.

But thou, O Hope, with eyes so fair,
What was thy delighted measure?

Still it whisper'd promised pleasure,
And bade the lovely scenes at distance hail!
Still would her touch the strain prolong;
And from the rocks, the woods, the vale,
She call'd on Echo still, through all the song;
And, where her sweetest theme she chose,
A soft responsive voice was heard at every close,
And Hope enchanted smiled, and waved her golden hair.
And longer had she sung; but, with a frown,
Revenge impatient rose:
He threw his blood-stain'd sword, in thunder, down;
And, with a withering look,
The war-denouncing trumpet took,
And blew a blast so loud and dread,
Were ne'er prophetic sounds so full of woe!
And, ever and anon, he beat
The doubling drum, with furious heat;
And though sometimes, each dreary pause between,
Dejected Pity, at his side,
Her soul-subduing voice applied,
Yet still he kept his wild unalter'd mein,
While each strain'd ball of sight seem'd bursting from his head.
Thy numbers, Jealousy, to nought were fix'd;
Sad proof of thy distressful state;
Of differing themes the veering song was mix'd;
And now it courted Love, now raving call'd on Hate.

With eyes upraised, as one inspired,
Pale Melancholy sate retired;
And, from her wild sequester'd seat,
In notes by distance made more sweet,
Pour'd through the mellow horn her pensive soul:
And, dashing soft from rocks around,
Bubbling runnels join'd the sound;
Through glades and glooms the mingled measure stole,
Or, o'er some haunted stream, with fond delay,
Round an holy calm diffusing,
Love of Peace, and lonely musing,
In hollow murmurs died away.

But O! how alter'd was its sprightlier tone,
When Cheerfulness, a nymph of healthiest hue,
Her bow across her shoulder flung,
Her buskins gemm'd with morning dew,
Blew an inspiring air, that dale and thicket rung,
The hunter's call, to Faun and Dryad known!
The oak-crown'd Sisters, and their chaste-eyed Queen,
Satyrs and Sylvan Boys, were seen,
Peeping from forth their alleys green:
Brown Exercise rejoiced to hear;
And Sport leapt up, and seized his beechen spear.

Last came Joy's ecstatic trial:
He, with viny crown advancing,
First to the lively pipe his hand addrest;
But soon he saw the brisk awakening viol,
Whose sweet entrancing voice he loved the best;
They would have thought who heard the strain
They saw, in Tempe's vale, her native maids,
Amidst the festal sounding shades,
To some unwearied minstrel dancing,
While, as his flying fingers kiss'd the strings,
Love framed with Mirth a gay fantastic round:
Loose were her tresses seen, her zone unbound;
And he, amidst his frolic play,
As if he would the charming air repay,
Shook thousand odours from his dewy wings.

O Music! sphere-descended maid,
Friend of Pleasure, Wisdom's aid!
Why, goddess! why, to us denied,
Lay'st thou thy ancient lyre aside?
As, in that loved Athenian bower,
You learn'd an all commanding power,
Thy mimic soul, O Nymph endear'd,
Can well recall what then it heard;
Where is thy native simple heart,
Devote to Virtue, Fancy, Art?
Arise, as in that elder time,
Warm, energetic, chaste, sublime!
Thy wonders, in that godlike age,
Fill thy recording Sister's page
'Tis said, and I believe the tale,
Thy humblest reed could more prevail,
Had more of strength, diviner rage,
Than all which charms this laggard age;
E'en all at once together found,
Cecilia's mingled world of sound
O bid our vain endeavours cease;
Revive the just designs of Greece:
Return in all thy simple state!
Confirm the tales her sons relate!

ODE ON THE DEATH OF THOMSON.

THE SCENE IS SUPPOSED TO LIE ON THE THAMES NEAR RICHMOND.

In yonder grave a Druid lies,
Where slowly winds the stealing wave;
The year's best sweets shall duteous rise
To deck its poet's sylvan grave.

In yon deep bed of whispering reeds
His airy harp shall now be laid,
That he, whose heart in sorrow bleeds,
May love through life the soothing shade.

Then maids and youths shall linger here,
And while its sounds at distance swell,
Shall sadly seem in pity's ear
To hear the woodland pilgrim's knell.

Remembrance oft shall haunt the shore
When Thames in summer wreaths is drest,
And oft suspend the dashing oar,
To bid his gentle spirit rest!

And oft, as ease and health retire
To breezy lawn, or forest deep,
The friend shall view yon whitening spire
And 'mid the varied landscape weep.

But thou, who own'st that earthy bed,
Ah! what will every dirge avail;
Or tears, which love and pity shed,
That mourn beneath the gliding sail?

Yet lives there one, whose heedless eye
Shall scorn thy pale shrine glimmering near?
With him, sweet bard, may fancy die,
And joy desert the blooming year.

But thou, lorn stream, whose sullen tide
No sedge-crown'd sisters now attend,
Now waft me from the green hill's side,
Whose cold turf hides the buried friend!

And see, the fairy valleys fade;
Dun night has veil'd the solemn view!
Yet once again, dear parted shade,
Meek Nature's Child, again adieu!

The genial meads, assign'd to bless
Thy life, shall mourn thy early doom;
Their hinds and shepherd-girls shall dress,
With simple hands, thy rural tomb.

Long, long, thy stone and pointed clay
Shall melt the musing Briton's eyes:
O! vales and wild woods, shall he say,
In yonder grave your Druid lies!

ODE ON THE POPULAR SUPERSTITIONS OF THE HIGHLANDS OF SCOTLAND;
CONSIDERED AS THE SUBJECT OF POETRY; INSCRIBED TO MR. JOHN HOME.

I.

Home, thou return'st from Thames, whose Naiads long
Have seen thee lingering with a fond delay,
'Mid those soft friends, whose hearts, some future day,
Shall melt, perhaps, to hear thy tragic song.
Go, not unmindful of that cordial youth
Whom, long endear'd, thou leavest by Levant's side;
Together let us wish him lasting truth,
And joy untainted with his destined bride.
Go! nor regardless, while these numbers boast
My short-lived bliss, forget my social name;
But think, far off, how, on the southern coast,
I met thy friendship with an equal flame!
Fresh to that soil thou turn'st, where every vale
Shall prompt the poet, and his song demand:
To thee thy copious subjects ne'er shall fail;
Thou need'st but take thy pencil to thy hand,
And paint what all believe, who own thy genial land.

II.

There must thou wake perforce thy Doric quill;
'Tis Fancy's land to which thou sett'st thy feet;
Where still, 'tis said, the fairy people meet,
Beneath each birken shade, on mead or hill;
There, each trim lass, that skims the milky store,
To the swart tribes their creamy bowls allots;
By night they sip it round the cottage door,
While airy minstrels warble jocund notes.
There, every herd, by sad experience, knows
How, wing'd with fate, their elf-shot arrows fly,
When the sick ewe her summer food foregoes,
Or, stretch'd on earth, the heart-smit heifers lie.
Such airy beings awe the untutor'd swain:
Nor thou, though learn'd, his homelier thoughts neglect;
Let thy sweet muse the rural faith sustain;
These are the themes of simple, sure effect,
That add new conquests to her boundless reign,
And fill, with double force, her heart-commanding strain.

III.

E'en yet preserved, how often mayst thou hear,
Where to the pole the Boreal mountains run,
Taught by the father, to his listening son,
Strange lays, whose power had charm'd a Spenser's ear.
At every pause, before thy mind possest,
Old Runic bards shall seem to rise around,

With uncouth lyres, in many-colour'd vest,
Their matted hair with boughs fantastic crown'd:
Whether thou bidst the well taught hind repeat
The choral dirge, that mourns some chieftain brave,
When every shrieking maid her bosom beat,
And strew'd with choicest herbs his scented grave!
Or whether, sitting in the shepherd's shiel,
Thou hear'st some sounding tale of war's alarms;
When at the bugle's call, with fire and steel,
The sturdy clans pour'd forth their brawny swarms,
And hostile brothers met, to prove each other's arms.

IV.
'Tis thine to sing, how, framing hideous spells,
In Sky's lone isle, the gifted wizard seer,
Lodged in the wintry cave with Fate's fell spear,
Or in the depth of Uist's dark forest dwells:
How they, whose sight such dreary dreams engross,
With their own visions oft astonish'd droop,
When, o'er the watery strath, or quaggy moss,
They see the gliding ghosts unbodied troop.
Or, if in sports, or on the festive green,
Their destined glance some fated youth descry,
Who now, perhaps, in lusty vigour seen,
And rosy health, shall soon lamented die.
For them the viewless forms of air obey;
Their bidding heed, and at their beck repair:
They know what spirit brews the stormful day,
And heartless, oft like moody madness, stare
To see the phantom train their secret work prepare.

V.
To monarchs dear, some hundred miles astray,
Oft have they seen Fate give the fatal blow!
The seer, in Sky, shriek'd as the blood did flow,
When headless Charles warm on the scaffold lay!
As Boreas threw his young Aurora forth,
In the first year of the first George's reign,
And battles raged in welkin of the North,
They mourn'd in air, fell, fell Rebellion slain!
And as, of late, they joy'd in Preston's fight,
Saw, at sad Falkirk, all their hopes near crown'd!
They raved! divining, through their second sight,
Pale, red Culloden, where these hopes were drown'd!
Illustrious William! Britain's guardian name!
One William saved us from a tyrant's stroke;
He, for a sceptre, gain'd heroic fame,
But thou, more glorious, Slavery's chain hast broke,
To reign a private man, and bow to Freedom's yoke!

VI.

These, too, thou'lt sing! for well thy magic muse
Can to the topmost heaven of grandeur soar;
Or stoop to wail the swain that is no more!
Ah, homely swains! your homeward steps ne'er lose;
Let not dank Will mislead you to the heath;
Dancing in mirky night, o'er fen and lake,
He glows, to draw you downward to your death,
In his bewitch'd, low, marshy, willow brake!
What though far off, from some dark dell espied,
His glimmering mazes cheer the excursive sight,
Yet turn, ye wanderers, turn your steps aside,
Nor trust the guidance of that faithless light;
For watchful, lurking, 'mid the unrustling reed,
At those mirk hours the wily monster lies,
And listens oft to hear the passing steed,
And frequent round him rolls his sullen eyes,
If chance his savage wrath may some weak wretch surprise.

VII.
Ah, luckless swain, o'er all unblest, indeed!
Whom late bewilder'd in the dank, dark fen,
Far from his flocks, and smoking hamlet, then!
To that sad spot where hums the sedgy weed:
On him, enraged, the fiend, in angry mood,
Shall never look with pity's kind concern,
But instant, furious, raise the whelming flood
O'er its drown'd banks, forbidding all return!
Or, if he meditate his wish'd escape,
To some dim hill, that seems uprising near,
To his faint eye the grim and grisly shape,
In all its terrors clad, shall wild appear.   1
Meantime the watery surge shall round him rise,
Pour'd sudden forth from every swelling source!
What now remains but tears and hopeless sighs?
His fear-shook limbs have lost their youthly force,
And down the waves he floats, a pale and breathless corse!

VIII.
For him in vain his anxious wife shall wait,
Or wander forth to meet him on his way;
For him in vain at to-fall of the day,
His babes shall linger at the unclosing gate!
Ah, ne'er shall he return! Alone, if night
Her travel'd limbs in broken slumbers steep,
With drooping willows drest, his mournful sprite
Shall visit sad, perchance, her silent sleep:
Then he, perhaps, with moist and watery hand,
Shall fondly seem to press her shuddering cheek,
And with his blue swoln face before her stand,
And, shivering cold, these piteous accents speak:
"Pursue, dear wife, thy daily toils pursue,

At dawn or dusk, industrious as before;
Nor e'er of me one helpless thought renew,
While I lie weltering on the osier'd shore,
Drown'd by the Kelpie's wrath, nor e'er shall aid thee more!"

IX.
Unbounded is thy range; with varied skill
Thy muse may, like those feathery tribes which spring
From their rude rocks, extend her skirting wing
Round the moist marge of each cold Hebrid isle,
To that hoar pile which still its ruins shows:
In whose small vaults a pigmy folk is found,
Whose bones the delver with his spade upthrows,
And culls them, wondering, from the hallow'd ground!
Or thither, where, beneath the showery west,
The mighty kings of three fair realms are laid;
Once foes, perhaps, together now they rest,
No slaves revere them, and no wars invade:
Yet frequent now, at midnight's solemn hour,
The rifted mounds their yawning cells unfold,
And forth the monarchs stalk with sovereign power,
In pageant robes, and wreath'd with sheeny gold,
And on their twilight tombs aërial council hold.

X.
But, oh, o'er all, forget not Kilda's race,
On whose bleak rocks, which brave the wasting tides,
Fair Nature's daughter, Virtue, yet abides.
Go! just, as they, their blameless manners trace!
Then to my ear transmit some gentle song,
Of those whose lives are yet sincere and plain,
Their bounded walks the rugged cliffs along,
And all their prospect but the wintry main.
With sparing temperance, at the needful time,
They drain the scented spring; or, hunger-prest,
Along the Atlantic rock, undreading climb,
And of its eggs despoil the solan's nest.
Thus, blest in primal innocence, they live
Sufficed, and happy with that frugal fare
Which tasteful toil and hourly danger give.
Hard is their shallow soil, and bleak and bare;
Nor ever vernal bee was heard to murmur there!

XI.
Nor need'st thou blush that such false themes engage
Thy gentle mind, of fairer stores possest;
For not alone they touch the village breast,
But fill'd, in elder time, the historic page.
There, Shakespeare's self, with every garland crown'd,
Flew to those fairy climes his fancy sheen,
In musing hour; his wayward sisters found,

And with their terrors drest the magic scene.
From them he sung, when, 'mid his bold design,
Before the Scot, afflicted, and aghast!
The shadowy kings of Banquo's fated line
Through the dark cave in gleamy pageant pass'd.
Proceed! nor quit the tales which, simply told,
Could once so well my answering bosom pierce;
Proceed, in forceful sounds, and colours bold,
The native legends of thy land rehearse;
To such adapt thy lyre, and suit thy powerful verse.

XII.
In scenes like these, which, daring to depart
From sober truth, are still to nature true,
And call forth fresh delight to Fancy's view,
The heroic muse employ'd her Tasso's art!
How have I trembled, when, at Tancred's stroke,
Its gushing blood the gaping cypress pour'd!
When each live plant with mortal accents spoke,
And the wild blast upheaved the vanish'd sword!
How have I sat, when piped the pensive wind,
To hear his harp by British Fairfax strung!
Prevailing poet! whose undoubting mind
Believed the magic wonders which he sung!
Hence, at each sound, imagination glows!
Hence, at each picture, vivid life starts here!
Hence his warm lay with softest sweetness flows!
Melting it flows, pure, murmuring, strong, and clear,
And fills the impassion'd heart, and wins the harmonious ear!

XIII.
All hail, ye scenes that o'er my soul prevail!
Ye splendid friths and lakes, which, far away,
Are by smooth Annan fill'd or pastoral Tay,
Or Don's romantic springs at distance hail!
The time shall come, when I, perhaps, may tread
Your lowly glens, o'erhung with spreading broom;
Or, o'er your stretching heaths, by Fancy led;
Or, o'er your mountains creep, in awful gloom!
Then will I dress once more the faded bower,
Where Jonson sat in Drummond's classic shade;
Or crop, from Tiviotdale, each lyric flower,
And mourn, on Yarrow's banks, where Willy's laid!
Meantime, ye powers that on the plains which bore
The cordial youth, on Lothian's plains, attend!
Where'er Home dwells, on hill, or lowly moor,
To him I lose, your kind protection lend,
And, touch'd with love like mine, preserve my absent friend!

AN EPISTLE, ADDRESSED TO SIR THOMAS HANMER, ON HIS EDITION OF SHAKESPEARE'S WORKS.

SIR,
A patriot's hand protects a poet's lays,
While nursed by you she sees her myrtles bloom,
Green and unwither'd o'er his honour'd tomb;
Excuse her doubts, if yet she fears to tell
What secret transports in her bosom swell:
With conscious awe she hears the critic's fame,
And blushing hides her wreath at Shakespeare's name.
Hard was the lot those injured strains endured,
Unown'd by Science, and by years obscured:
Fair Fancy wept; and echoing sighs confess'd
A fix'd despair in every tuneful breast.
Not with more grief the afflicted swains appear,
When wintry winds deform the plenteous year;
When lingering frosts the ruin'd seats invade
Where Peace resorted, and the Graces play'd.

Each rising art by just gradation moves,
Toil builds on toil, and age on age improves:
The Muse alone unequal dealt her rage,
And graced with noblest pomp her earliest stage.
Preserved through time, the speaking scenes impart
Each changeful wish of Phædra's tortured heart;
Or paint the curse that mark'd the Theban's reign,
A bed incestuous, and a father slain.
With kind concern our pitying eyes o'erflow,
Trace the sad tale, and own another's woe.

To Rome removed, with wit secure to please,
The comic Sisters kept their native ease:
With jealous fear, declining Greece beheld
Her own Menander's art almost excell'd;
But every Muse essay'd to raise in vain
Some labour'd rival of her tragic strain:
Ilissus' laurels, though transferr'd with toil,
Droop'd their fair leaves, nor knew the unfriendly soil.
As Arts expired, resistless Dulness rose;
Goths, Priests, or Vandals, all were Learning's foes.
Till Julius first recall'd each exiled maid,
And Cosmo own'd them in the Etrurian shade:
Then, deeply skill'd in love's engaging theme,
The soft Provençal pass'd to Arno's stream:
With graceful ease the wanton lyre he strung;
Sweet flow'd the lays but love was all he sung.
The gay description could not fail to move,
For, led by nature, all are friends to love.

But Heaven, still various in its works, decreed
The perfect boast of time should last succeed.

The beauteous union must appear at length,
Of Tuscan fancy, and Athenian strength:
One greater Muse Eliza's reign adorn,
And e'en a Shakespeare to her fame be born!

Yet ah! so bright her morning's opening ray,
In vain our Britain hoped an equal day!
No second growth the western isle could bear,
At once exhausted with too rich a year.
Too nicely Jonson knew the critic's part;
Nature in him was almost lost in art.
Of softer mould the gentle Fletcher came,
The next in order, as the next in name;
With pleased attention, 'midst his scenes we find
Each glowing thought that warms the female mind;
Each melting sigh, and every tender tear;
The lover's wishes, and the virgin's fear.
His every strain the Smiles and Graces own;
But stronger Shakespeare felt for man alone:
Drawn by his pen, our ruder passions stand
The unrival'd picture of his early hand.

With gradual steps and slow, exacter France
Saw Art's fair empire o'er her shores advance:
By length of toil a bright perfection knew,
Correctly bold, and just in all she drew:
Till late Corneille, with Lucan's spirit fired,
Breathed the free strain, as Rome and he inspired:
And classic judgment gain'd to sweet Racine
The temperate strength of Maro's chaster line.

But wilder far the British laurel spread,
And wreaths less artful crown our poet's head.
Yet he alone to every scene could give
The historian's truth, and bid the manners live.
Waked at his call I view, with glad surprise,
Majestic forms of mighty monarchs rise.
There Henry's trumpets spread their loud alarms,
And laurel'd Conquest waits her hero's arms.
Here gentler Edward claims a pitying sigh,
Scarce born to honours, and so soon to die!
Yet shall thy throne, unhappy infant, bring
No beam of comfort to the guilty king:
The time shall come when Glo'ster's heart shall bleed,
In life's last hours, with horror of the deed;
When dreary visions shall at last present
Thy vengeful image in the midnight tent:
Thy hand unseen the secret death shall bear,
Blunt the weak sword, and break the oppressive spear!

Where'er we turn, by Fancy charm'd, we find

Some sweet illusion of the cheated mind.
Oft, wild of wing, she calls the soul to rove
With humbler nature, in the rural grove;
Where swains contented own the quiet scene,
And twilight fairies tread the circled green:
Dress'd by her hand, the woods and valleys smile,
And Spring diffusive decks the enchanted isle.

O, more than all in powerful genius blest,
Come, take thine empire o'er the willing breast!
Whate'er the wounds this youthful heart shall feel,
Thy songs support me, and thy morals heal!
There every thought the poet's warmth may raise,
There native music dwells in all the lays.
O might some verse with happiest skill persuade
Expressive Picture to adopt thine aid!
What wondrous draughts might rise from every page!
What other Raphaels charm a distant age!

Methinks e'en now I view some free design,
Where breathing Nature lives in every line:
Chaste and subdued the modest lights decay,
Steal into shades, and mildly melt away.
And see where Anthony, in tears approved,
Guards the pale relics of the chief he loved:
O'er the cold corse the warrior seems to bend,
Deep sunk in grief, and mourns his murder'd friend!
Still as they press, he calls on all around,
Lifts the torn robe, and points the bleeding wound.

But who is he, whose brows exalted bear
A wrath impatient, and a fiercer air?
Awake to all that injured worth can feel,
On his own Rome he turns the avenging steel;
Yet shall not war's insatiate fury fall
(So heaven ordains it) on the destined wall.
See the fond mother, 'midst the plaintive train,
Hung on his knees, and prostrate on the plain!
Touch'd to the soul, in vain he strives to hide
The son's affection, in the Roman's pride:
O'er all the man conflicting passions rise;
Rage grasps the sword, while Pity melts the eyes.

Thus generous Critic, as thy Bard inspires,
The sister Arts shall nurse their drooping fires;
Each from his scenes her stores alternate bring,
Blend the fair tints, or wake the vocal string:
Those sibyl leaves, the sport of every wind,
(For poets ever were a careless kind,)
By thee disposed, no farther toil demand,
But, just to Nature, own thy forming hand.

So spread o'er Greece, the harmonious whole unknown,
E'en Homer's numbers charm'd by parts alone.
Their own Ulysses scarce had wander'd more,
By winds and waters cast on every shore:
When, raised by fate, some former Hanmer join'd
Each beauteous image of the boundless mind;
And bade, like thee, his Athens ever claim
A fond alliance with the Poet's name.

Oxford, Dec. 3,
1743.

DIRGE IN CYMBELINE, SUNG BY GUIDERUS AND ARVIRAGUS OVER FIDELE, SUPPOSED TO BE DEAD.

To fair Fidele's grassy tomb
Soft maids and village hinds shall bring
Each opening sweet of earliest bloom,
And rifle all the breathing spring.

No wailing ghost shall dare appear
To vex with shrieks this quiet grove;
But shepherd lads assemble here,
And melting virgins own their love.

No wither'd witch shall here be seen;
No goblins lead their nightly crew:
The female fays shall haunt the green,
And dress thy grave with pearly dew!

The redbreast oft, at evening hours,
Shall kindly lend his little aid,
With hoary moss, and gather'd flowers,
To deck the ground where thou art laid.

When howling winds, and beating rain,
In tempests shake the sylvan cell;
Or 'midst the chase, on every plain,
The tender thought on thee shall dwell;

Each lonely scene shall thee restore;
For thee the tear be duly shed;
Beloved till life can charm no more,
And mourn'd till Pity's self be dead.

VERSES WRITTEN ON A PAPER WHICH CONTAINED A PIECE OF BRIDE-CAKE, GIVEN TO THE AUTHOR BY A LADY.

Ye curious hands, that, hid from vulgar eyes,
By search profane shall find this hallow'd cake,
With virtue's awe forbear the sacred prize,
Nor dare a theft, for love and pity's sake!

This precious relic, form'd by magic power,
Beneath her shepherd's haunted pillow laid,
Was meant by love to charm the silent hour,
The secret present of a matchless maid.

The Cyprian queen, at Hymen's fond request,
Each nice ingredient chose with happiest art;
Fears, sighs, and wishes of the enamour'd breast,
And pains that please, are mix'd in every part.

With rosy hand the spicy fruit she brought,
From Paphian hills, and fair Cythera's isle;
And temper'd sweet with these the melting thought,
The kiss ambrosial, and the yielding smile.

Ambiguous looks, that scorn and yet relent,
Denials mild, and firm unalter'd truth;
Reluctant pride, and amorous faint consent,
And meeting ardours, and exulting youth.

Sleep, wayward God! hath sworn, while these remain,
With flattering dreams to dry his nightly tear,
And cheerful Hope, so oft invoked in vain,
With fairy songs shall soothe his pensive ear.

If, bound by vows to Friendship's gentle side,
And fond of soul, thou hop'st an equal grace,
If youth or maid thy joys and griefs divide,
O, much entreated, leave this fatal place!

Sweet Peace, who long hath shunn'd my plaintive day,
Consents at length to bring me short delight,
Thy careless steps may scare her doves away,
And Grief with raven note usurp the night.

TO MISS AURELIA C----R, ON HER WEEPING AT HER SISTER'S WEDDING.

Cease, fair Aurelia, cease to mourn,
Lament not Hannah's happy state;
You may be happy in your turn,
And seize the treasure you regret.

With Love united Hymen stands,
And softly whispers to your charms,

"Meet but your lover in my bands,
You'll find your sister in his arms."

SONNET.

When Phœbe form'd a wanton smile,
My soul! it reach'd not here:
Strange, that thy peace, thou trembler, flies
Before a rising tear!
From 'midst the drops, my love is born,   5
That o'er those eyelids rove:
Thus issued from a teeming wave
The fabled queen of love.

SONG. THE SENTIMENTS BORROWED FROM SHAKESPEARE.

Young Damon of the vale is dead,
Ye lowly hamlets, moan;
A dewy turf lies o'er his head,
And at his feet a stone.

His shroud, which Death's cold damps destroy,
Of snow-white threads was made:
All mourn'd to see so sweet a boy
In earth for ever laid.

Pale pansies o'er his corpse were placed,
Which, pluck'd before their time,
Bestrew'd the boy, like him to waste
And wither in their prime.

But will he ne'er return, whose tongue
Could tune the rural lay?
Ah, no! his bell of peace is rung,
His lips are cold as clay.

They bore him out at twilight hour,
The youth who loved so well:
Ah, me! how many a true love shower
Of kind remembrance fell!

Each maid was woe but Lucy chief,
Her grief o'er all was tried;
Within his grave she dropp'd in grief,
And o'er her loved one died.

ON OUR LATE TASTE IN MUSIC.

Quid vocis modulamen inane juvabat
Verborum sensusque vacans numerique loquacis?
MILTON.

Britons! away with the degenerate pack!
Waft, western winds! the foreign spoilers back!
Enough has been in wild amusements spent,
Let British verse and harmony content!
No music once could charm you like your own,
Then tuneful Robinson, and Tofts were known;
Then Purcell touched the strings, while numbers hung
Attentive to the sounds and blest the song!
E'en gentle Weldon taught us manly notes,
Beyond the enervate thrills of Roman throats!
Notes, foreign luxury could ne'er inspire,
That animate the soul, and swell the lyre!
That mend, and not emasculate our hearts,
And teach the love of freedom and of arts.
Nor yet, while guardian Phœbus gilds our isle,
Does heaven averse await the muses' toil;
Cherish but once our worth of native race,
The sister-arts shall soon display their face!
Even half discouraged through the gloom they strive,
Smile at neglect, and o'er oblivion live.
See Handel, careless of a foreign fame,
Fix on our shore, and boast a Briton's name:
While, placed marmoric in the vocal grove,
He guides the measures listening throngs approve.
Mark silence at the voice of Arne confess'd,
Soft as the sweet enchantress rules the breast;
As when transported Venice lent an ear,
Camilla's charms to view, and accents hear!
So while she varies the impassion'd song,
Alternate motions on the bosom throng!
As heavenly Milton guides her magic voice,
And virtue thus convey'd allures the choice.
Discard soft nonsense in a slavish tongue,
The strain insipid, and the thought unknown;
From truth and nature form the unerring test;
Be what is manly, chaste, and good the best!
'Tis not to ape the songsters of the groves,
Through all the quiverings of their wanton loves;
'Tis not the enfeebled thrill, or warbled shake,
The heart can strengthen, or the soul awake!
But where the force of energy is found
When the sense rises on the wings of sound;
When reason, with the charms of music twined,
Through the enraptured ear informs the mind;
Bids generous love or soft compassion glow,
And forms a tuneful Paradise below!

Oh Britons! if the honour still you boast,
No longer purchase follies at such cost!
No longer let unmeaning sounds invite
To visionary scenes of false delight:
When, shame to sense! we see the hero's rage
Lisp'd on the tongue, and danced along the stage!
Or hear in eunuch sounds a hero squeak,
While kingdoms rise or fall upon a shake!
Let them at home to slavery's painted train,
With siren art, repeat the pleasing strain:
While we, like wise Ulysses, close our ear
To songs which liberty forbids to hear!
Keep, guardian gales, the infectious guests away,
To charm where priests direct, and slaves obey.
Madrid, or wanton Rome, be their delight;
There they may warble as their poets write.
The temper of our isle, though cold, is clear;
And such our genius, noble though severe.
Our Shakespeare scorn'd the trifling rules of art,
But knew to conquer and surprise the heart!
In magic chains the captive thought to bind,
And fathom all the depths of human kind!
Too long, our shame, the prostituted herd
Our sense have bubbled, and our wealth have shared.
Too long the favourites of our vulgar great
Have bask'd in luxury, and lived in state!
In Tuscan wilds now let them villas rear
Ennobled by the charity we spare.
There let them warble in the tainted breeze,
Or sing like widow'd orphans to the trees:
There let them chant their incoherent dreams,
Where howls Charybdis, and where Scylla screams!
Or where Avernus, from his darksome round,
May echo to the winds the blasted sound!
As fair Alcyone, with anguish press'd,
Broods o'er the British main with tuneful breast,
Beneath the white-brow'd cliff protected sings,
Or skims the azure plain with painted wings!
Grateful, like her, to nature, and as just,
In our domestic blessings let us trust;
Keep for our sons fair learning's honour'd prize,
Till the world own the worth they now despise!

AN ESSAY ON THE GENIUS AND POEMS OF COLLINS.
BY SIR EGERTON BRYDGES, BART.

Collins is the founder of a new school of poetry, of a high class. It is true that, unless Buckhurst and Spenser had gone before him, he could not have written as he has done; yet he is an inventor very distinct from both. He calls his odes descriptive and allegorical; and this characterises them truly, but too generally. The personification of abstract qualities had never been so happily executed before; the pure spirituality of the conception, the elegance and force of the language, the harmony and variety of the numbers, were all executed with a felicity which none before or since have reached. That these poems did not at once captivate the public attention cannot be accounted for by any cause hitherto assigned. We may not wonder that the multitude did not at once perceive their full beauties; but that, among readers of taste and learning, there should not have been found a sufficient number to set the example of admiration, is very extraordinary. In addition to all their other high merits, the mere novelty of thought and manner were sufficient to excite immediate notice. Nor was there any thing in Collins's station or character to create prejudices against the probability that beautiful effusions of genius might be struck out by his hand. His education at the college of Winchester, his fame at Oxford, his associates in London, all were fair preludes to the production of beautiful poetry. Indeed, he had already produced beautiful poetry in his Oriental Eclogues, four years before his Odes appeared. These were, it is admitted, of a different cast from his Odes, and of a gentleness and chastity of thought and diction, which he himself was conscious, some years afterwards, did not very well represent the gorgeousness of eastern composition.

It was a crisis when there was a fair opening for new candidates for the laurel. The uniformity of Pope's style began already to pall upon the public ear. Thomson was indolent, and Young eccentric; Gray had not yet appeared on the stage; and Akenside's metaphysical subject and diffuse style were not calculated to engross the general taste. Johnson had taken possession of the field of satire, but there are too many readers of enthusiastic mind to be satisfied with satire. The pedantry and uncouthness of Walter Harte had precluded him from ever being a favourite with the public; Shenstone had not yet risen into fame; and Lyttelton was engrossed by politics. When, therefore, Collins's Odes appeared, all speculation would have anticipated that they must have been successful. But we must recollect that they did not excite the admiration of Johnson; and that Gray did not read them with that unqualified approval which his native taste would have inspired. This singularity must be accounted for by other causes than their want of merit.

The disappointment of Collins was so keen and deep, that he not only burned the unsold copies with his own hand, but soon fell into a melancholy which ended in insanity. Many persons have affected to comment on this result with an unfeeling ignorance of human nature, and, more especially, of fervid genius. It is, undoubtedly, highly dangerous to give the entire reins to imagination; the discipline of a constant exercise of reason is not only salutary, but necessary. But one can easily conceive how the indulgence of that state of mind which produced Collins's Odes could end in an entire overthrow of the intellect, when embittered by a defect of the principal objects of his worldly ambition. He is said to have been puffed up by a vanity which prompted him to expect that all eyes would be upon him, and all voices lifted in his praise. Such was the conception of a vulgar observer of the human character. Why should it have been vanity that prompted this hope? It was a consciousness of merit, of those brilliant powers which produced the Ode to the Passions! was ever a voice content which sung to those who would not hear, which was condemned

"To waste its sweetness on the desert air?"

Spenser's power of personification is copious beyond example; but it is seldom sufficiently select; rich as it is in imagination, it too commonly wants taste and delicacy; it has the fault of coarseness, which Burke's images in prose two centuries afterwards, sometimes fell into. But Collins's images are as pure, and of as exquisite delicacy, as they are spiritual. They are not human beings invested with some of the attributes of angels, but the whole figure is purely angelic, and of a higher order of creation; in this they are distinct even from the admirable personifications of Gray, because they are less earthly. The Ode to the Passions is, by universal consent, the noblest of Collins's productions, because it exhibits a much more extended invention, not of one passion only, but of all the passions combined, acting, according to the powers of each, to one end. The execution, also, is the happiest, each particular passion is drawn with inimitable force and compression. Let us take only FEAR and DESPAIR, each dashed out in four lines, of which every word is like inspiration. Beautiful as Spenser is, and sometimes sublime, yet he redoubles his touches too much, and often introduces some coarse feature or expression, which destroys the spell. Spenser, indeed, has other merits of splendid and inexhaustible invention, which render it impossible to put Collins on a par with him: but we must not estimate merit by mere quantity: if a poet produces but one short piece, which is perfect, he must be placed according to its quality. And surely there is not a single figure in Collins's Ode to the Passions which is not perfect, both in conception and language. He has had many imitators, but no one has ever approached him in his own department.

The Ode to Evening is, perhaps, the next in point of merit. It is quite of a different cast; it is descriptive of natural scenery; and such a scene of enchanting repose was never exhibited by Claude, or any other among the happiest of painters. Though a mere verbal description can never rival a fine picture in a mere address to the material part of our nature, yet it far eclipses it with those who have the endowment of a brilliant fancy, because it gratifies their taste, selection, and sentiment. Delightful, therefore, as it is to look upon a Claude, it is more delightful to look upon this description. It is vain to attempt to analyse the charm of this Ode; it is so subtle, that it escapes analysis. Its harmony is so perfect, that it requires no rhyme: the objects are so happily chosen, and the simple epithets convey ideas and feelings so congenial to each other, as to throw the reader into the very mood over which the personified being so beautifully designed presides. No other poem on the same subject has the same magic. It assuredly suggested some images and a tone of expression to Gray in his Elegy.

The Ode on the Poetical Character is here and there a little involved and obscure; but its general conception is magnificent, and beaming that spirit of inventive enthusiasm, which alone can cherish the poet's powers, and bring forth the due fruits. Collins never touched the lyre but he was borne away by the inspiration under which he laboured. The Dirge in Cymbeline, the lines on Thomson, and the Ode on Colonel Ross breathe such a beautiful simplicity of pathos, and yet are so highly poetical and graceful in every thought and tone, that, exquisitely polished as they are, and without one superfluous or one prosaic word, they never once betray the artifices of composition. The extreme transparency of the words and thoughts would induce a vulgar reader to consider them trite, while they are the expression of a genius so refined as to be all essence of spirit. In Gray, excellent as he is, we continually encounter the marks of labour and effort, and occasional crudeness, which shows that effort had not always succeeded, such as "iron hand and torturing hour;" but nothing of this kind occurs in the principal poems of Collins. There is a fire of mind which supersedes labour, and produces what labour cannot. It has been said that Collins is neither sublime nor pathetic; but only ingenious and fanciful. The truth is, that he was cast in the very mould of sublimity and pathos. He lived in an atmosphere above the earth, and breathed only in a visionary world. He was conversant with nothing else, and this must have been the secret by which he produced compositions so entirely spiritual. He who has daily intercourse with the world, and feels the vulgar human passions, cannot be in a humour to write poems which do not partake of earthly coarseness.

It may be asked, cui bono? what is the moral use of such poems as these? Whatever refines the intellect improves the heart; whatever augments and fortifies the spiritual part of our nature raises us in the rank of created beings. And what poems are more calculated to refine our intellect, and increase our spirituality, than the poems of Collins? To embody, in a brilliant manner, the most beautiful abstractions, to put them into action, and to add to them splendour, harmony, strength, and purity of language, is to complete a task as admirable for its use and its delight, as it is difficult to be executed. No one can receive the intellectual gratification which such works are capable of producing without being the better for it. The understanding was never yet roused to the conception of such pure and abstract thinking without an elevation of the whole nature of the being so roused. The expression of subtle and evanescent ideas, carried to its perfection, is among the very noblest and most exalted studies with which the human mind can be conversant.

It has been the fashion of our own age to beat out works into twentyfold and fiftyfold the size of those of Collins. I do not quarrel with that fashion; each fashion has its use: and my own taste induces me to perceive the value and many attractions of long narrative poems, full of human passions and practical wisdom. The matter is more desirable than the workmanship; and much of occasional carelessness in the language may be forgiven, for fertility of natural and just thought and interest of story. But this in no degree diminishes the value of those gems, which, though of the smallest size, comprehend perfections of every kind. It is easier to work upon a large field than a small one, one where is

"Ample room and verge enough
The characters of hell to trace."

But these diffuse productions are not calculated to give the same sort of pleasure as the gems. How difficult was the path chosen by Collins is sufficiently proved by the want of success of all who have entered the same walk: Gray's was not the same, as I shall endeavour presently to show. In the miscellany of Dodsley and other collectors will be found numerous attempts at Allegorical Odes: they are almost all nauseous failures, without originality or distinctness of conception; bald in their language, lame in their numbers, and repulsive from their insipidity of ideas.

Gray's personifications can scarcely be called allegorical, they have so much of humanity about them. He dealt in all the noble and melancholy feelings of the human heart: he never for one moment forgot to be a moralist: he was constantly under the influence of powerful sympathy for the miseries of man's life; and wrote from the overflow of his bosom rather than of his imagination. It is true that his imagination presented the pictures to him; but it was his heart which impelled him to speak. Take the Ode on the Prospect of Eton College; there is not one word which did not break from the bottom of his heart. The multitude cannot enter into the visionary world of Collins: all who have a spark of virtuous human feelings can sympathize with Gray. It is impossible to deny that of these two beautiful poets Gray is the most instructive as a moralist; but Gray is not so original as Collins, not so inventive, not so perfect in his language, and has not so much the fire and flow of inspiration.

When Collins is spoken of as one of the minor poets, it is a sad misapplication of the term. Unless he be minor because the number and size of his poems is small, no one is less a minor poet. In him every word is poetry, and poetry either sublime or pathetic. He does not rise to the sublimity of Milton or Dante, or reach the graceful tenderness of Petrarch; but he has a visionary invention of his own, to which there is no rival. As long as the language lasts, every richly gifted and richly cultivated mind will read him with intense and wondering rapture; and will not cease to entertain the conviction, from his example, if from no other, that true poetry of the higher orders is real inspiration. It will occur to many readers, on perusing these passages of exalted praise, that Johnson has spoken of Collins in a very different manner. Almost fifty years have elapsed since Johnson's final criticism on him appeared in his Lives of the Poets. It disgusted me so much at the time, and the disgust continued so violent, that for a long period it blinded me to all his stupendous merits, because it evinced not only bad taste but unamiable feelings. I cannot yet either justify it, or account for it. He speaks of Collins having sought for splendour without attaining it, of clogging his lines with consonants, and of mistaking inversion of language for poetry. Not one of these faults belongs to Collins. In almost all his poems the words follow their natural order, and are mellifluous beyond those of almost any other verse writer. If the Passions are not described with splendour, there is no such thing as splendour. If the beauties which he sought and attained are unnatural and extravagant, then the tests of correctness and good taste which have been hitherto set up must be abandoned. This severe criticism is the more extraordinary because Johnson professed a warm personal friendship for Collins; he professes admiration of his talents, learning, and taste, as well as of his disposition and heart, and speaks of his afflicting ill health with a passionate tenderness which has seldom been equalled in beauty, pathos, and force of language. That he could love him personally with such fondness, but be blind to his splendid and unrivaled genius, is utterly beyond my power to account for. Who can say that Johnson wanted taste when we read his sublime and acute criticisms on Milton, Dryden, and Pope? Was it that he roused all the faculties of his judgment when he spoke of these great men of past times; yet, that when he descended to his contemporaries, he indulged his feelings rather than his intellect, and suffered himself to be overcome by the evil passions of envy and contempt? His natural taste was, probably, not the best; when his criticisms were perfect he had tasked his intellect rather than his feelings. He was a man of general wisdom and undoubted genius, but not a very nice scholar, and he prided himself upon his every-day sense, his practical knowledge, rather than those visionary musings which he thought a dangerous indulgence of imagination. He could not put the compositions of Collins among the mere curiosities of literature, but he permitted himself to depreciate habits of mental excursion which he had not himself cultivated.

It was not till more than twenty years after Collins's death that his Ode on the Superstitions of the Highlands was recovered. The two Wartons had seen it, and spoke highly of it to Johnson and others. About 1781, or 1782, a copy was found among the papers of Dr. Carlysle, with a chasm of two or three stanzas. The public deemed it equal to the expectations which had been raised of it; for my part I will confess that I was always deeply disappointed at it. There are in it occasional traces of Collins's genius and several good lines, but none grand, none of that felicitous flow and inspired vigour which mark the Ode to the Passions and other of his lyrics, none of that happy personification of abstract conceptions which is the characteristic of his genius. The majority of the lines lag and move heavily, and do not seem to me to rise much above mediocrity in the expression. The subject was attractive, and might have afforded space for the wild excursions of Collins's creative powers. As to the edition of Bell, in which it is pretended that the lost stanzas have been recovered, I have no more doubt that they are spurious than that I did not write them myself: I will not dwell upon this subject, but only mention that it is quite impossible Collins could write "Fate gave the fatal blow," and "bowing to Freedom's yoke;" and such a line as

"In the first year of the first George's reign," &c.

There is not one line among these interpolated stanzas which it is possible that Collins could have written.

Mr. Ragdale relates that Collins was in the habit of writing numerous fragments, and then throwing them into the flames. Jackson, of Exeter, says the same of John Bampfylde. A sensitive mind is scarce ever satisfied with the reception it meets, when, in first heat of composition, it hopes to delight some listener, to which it first communicates its new effusions. It almost always considers itself to be "damn'd by faint praise." I have known fervid authors who, if they read or communicated a piece before it was finished, never went on with it. They thought it became blown upon, and turned from it with coldness, disgust, and despair. Yet the hearer is commonly not in fault: who can satisfy the warm hopes of aspiring and restless genius?

The Wartons have expressed themselves with praise and affection of Collins, but not, I think, with the entire admiration which was due to him. Joseph Warton was a good-natured and generous-minded man, but something of rivalry lurked in his bosom; and the fraternal partiality of Thomas

Warton had the same effect. The younger brother seems to have thought that Joseph's genius was equal to that of Collins. Gray had the critical acumen to discern the difference; but still he in no degree does justice to Collins. He accuses him of want of taste and selection, which is a surprising charge; and the more so, because Gray did not disdain to borrow from him. Gray's fault was an affected fastidiousness, as appears by the slighting manner in which he speaks of Thomson's Castle of Indolence on its first appearance, as well as of Akenside's Pleasures of Imagination, and Shenstone's Elegies. That Gray had exquisite taste, and was a perfect scholar, no one can doubt.

Collins lived thirteen years after the publication of his Odes. It does not appear that he produced any thing after this publication. How soon his grand mental malady extinguished his literary powers, I do not exactly know, nor is it recorded, whether any part of it arose from bodily disorders. Medical men have never agreed regarding this most deplorable of human afflictions. In Collins's case it probably arose from the mind. On such an intellectual temperament the extinction of the visions which Hope had painted to him seems to have been sufficient to produce that derangement, which first enfeebled, and then perverted and annihilated his faculties. The account given by Johnson is different from that supplied by Mr. Ragdale and another anonymous communication.

He had, perhaps, lucid intervals in which he discovered nothing but weakness and exhaustion. But he appears to have sometimes had fits of violence and despair. It seems that he was an enthusiastic admirer of Shakespeare, and a great reader of black letter books. It may be inferred that his studies were not entirely given up during his malady; but it is a subject of great wonder and regret that the Wartons, the intimate friends both of his better and darker days, have left no particular memorials of him. He had a sister, lately, if not still, living, from whom, though of a very uncongenial nature, something might surely have been gathered. But there is a familiarity which, by destroying admiration, destroys the perception of what will interest others. There are few of our poets of rare genius, of whose private life and character much is known. Little is known of Spenser, Shakespeare, and Milton: not much even of Thomson. More is known of Gray by the medium of his beautiful letters; but when Southey, Wordsworth, and Scott are gone, posterity will know every particular of them; and, even now, know much which fills them with delight and admiration. But let us know something in good time, also of the new candidates for poetical fame!

If the life of a poet is not in accordance with his song, it may be suspected that the song itself is not genuine. Who can be a poet, and yet be a worldling in his passions and habits? An artificial poet is a disgusting dealer in trifles: nothing but the predominance of strong and unstimulated feeling will give that inspiration without which it is worse than an empty sound. When the passion is factitious, the excitement has always an immoral tendency; but the delineation of real and amiable sentiments calls up a sympathy in other bosoms which thus confirms and fixes them where they would otherwise die away. The memory may preserve what is artificial, but, when it becomes stale, it turns to offensiveness, and thus breeds an alienation from literature itself.

That Collins has continued to increase in fame as years have passed away, is the most decisive of all proofs that his poems have the pure and sterling merit which began to be ascribed to them soon after his death. M. Bonstetten tells me that Gray died without a suspicion of the high rank he was thereafter to hold in the annals of British genius? What did poor Collins think when he submitted his sublime odes to the flames? He must have had fits of confidence, even then, in himself; but intermixed with gloom and despair, and curses of the wretched doom of his birth! Is it sufficient that a man should wrap himself up in himself, and be content if the poetry creates itself and expires in his own heart? We strike the lyre to excite sympathy, and, if no one will hear, will any one not feel that he strikes in vain; and that the talent given us is useless, and even painful? But who can be assured that he has the talent if no one acknowledges it? To have it, and not to be assured that we have it, is a restless fire that burns to consume us.

Let no one envy the endowments, if he looks at the fate, of poets. Let him contemplate Spenser, Denham, Rochester, Otway, Collins, Chatterton, Burns, Kirke White, Bloomfield, Shelley, Keats, and Byron, besides those of foreign countries! Perhaps Collins was the most unhappy of all; as he was assuredly one of the most inspired and most amiable.

"In woful measures wan Despair
Low sullen sounds his grief beguiled,
A solemn, strange, and mingled air;
'Twas sad by fits, by starts 'twas wild."

Langhorne's edition of Collins first appeared in 1765, accompanied by observations which have been generally appended to subsequent editions. These observations have commonly borne the character of feebleness and affectation; they have a sort of pedantic prettiness, which is somewhat repulsive, but they do not want ingenuity, or justness of criticism. Part of them, at least, had previously appeared in the Monthly Review, probably written by Langhorne. Langhorne was not deficient himself in poetical genius, but is principally remembered by a single beautiful stanza, "Cold on Canadian hills," &c. From the time of Langhorne's first edition, Collins became a popular poet; a miniature edition appeared soon after that of Langhorne; and as long as I can remember books, which goes back at least to the year 1770, Collins's poems were almost universally on the lips of readers of English poetry. That Cowper, in 1784, should speak of him as "a poet of no great fame," proves nothing, since Cowper's long seclusion from the world had made him utterly ignorant of contemporary literature. The negative inference, from the omission of Beattie, is not of much weight. I cannot recollect the date of the article in the Monthly Review; but, as it appears that Collins survived till 1759, I suspect it was before Collins's death. It was in September, 1754, that the Wartons visited him at Chichester: in that year he paid a visit to Oxford, when it appears that he was suffering under exhausture, not alienation, of mind.

The critics, and, among the rest, Mrs. Barbauld and Campbell, have ascribed to him "frequent obscurity;" this is unjust, his general characteristic is lucidness and transparency: he is never obscure, unless in the Ode to Liberty, and, perhaps, in a few passages of the Ode on the Manners. Campbell's criticism is, otherwise, worthy of this beautiful poet, whom he praises with congenial spirit. When Hazlitt speaks of the "tinsel and splendid patchwork" of Collins, "mixed with the solid, sterling ore of his genius," he speaks of a base material not to be found there. In Collins there is no tinsel or patchwork, one of his excellencies is, that the whole of every piece is of one web; there are no joinings or meaner threads. There is no height to which Collins might not have risen, had he lived long, had his mind continued sound, and had he persevered in exercising his genius. Campbell remarks that, at the same age, Milton had written nothing which could eclipse his productions.

Of the two communications regarding Collins, to which I have already alluded, one anonymous, the other by a Mr. John Ragsdale, I must say something more. The first, signed V., appeared in the Gentleman's Magazine, with the date of the 20th Jan. 1781. I well remember its publication, and with what eagerness I read it. I suspect it was at the very crisis of the appearance of the last portion of Johnson's Lives, but possibly a year earlier. I perused it with a mixture of delight, melancholy, and disgust; the first passage which struck me was this: "As he brought with him [to Oxford], for so the whole tone of his conversation discovered, too high an opinion of his school acquisitions and a sovereign contempt for all academic studies and discipline, he never looked with any complacency on his situation in the University, but was always complaining of the dulness of a college life. In short, he threw up his demyship, and going to London, commenced a man of the town, spending his time in all the dissipation of Ranelagh, Vauxhall, and the playhouses; and was romantic enough to suppose that his superior abilities would draw the attention of the great world, by means of whom he was to make his fortune," &c., &c. "Thus was lost to the world this unfortunate person, in the prime of life, without availing himself of fine abilities, which, if properly improved, must have raised him to the top of any profession, and have rendered him a blessing to his friends, and an ornament to his country."

The vulgarity and narrow-mindedness of this last paragraph filled me with indignation and contempt. In a selfish point of view Collins might, unquestionably, have done better by binding himself to the trammels of a profession; but would he have been more an honor to his friends and an ornament to his country? Are the fruits of genius he has left behind no ornament or use to his country? Professional men, for the most part, live for themselves, and not for the world. Who now remembers Lord Camden, Lord Thurlow, Lord Rosslyn, Lord Kenyon, Lord Ellenborough, or a hundred episcopal or medical characters, all rich and famous in their day?

The character of his person and habits we read with deep interest. "He was passionately fond of music, good-natured, and affable, warm in his friendships, and visionary in his pursuits; and, as long as I knew him, very temperate in his eating and drinking. He was of a moderate stature, of a light and clear complexion, with gray eyes, so very weak at times as hardly to bear a candle in the room, and often raising within him apprehensions of blindness."

The letter from Mr. John Ragsdale is addressed to Mr. William Hymers, Queen's College, Oxford, dated "Hill Street, Richmond, in Surrey, July, 1783." He appears to have been a tradesman in Bond Street; and he surveyed the character of Collins (with whom he was familiar) with a tradesman's eye. He reproached the poet with idleness, not because he was lingering and losing his time on the road to fame, but because he omitted to get money by his pen. "To raise a present subsistence," says Ragsdale, "he set about writing his Odes; and having a general invitation to my house, he frequently passed whole days there, which he employed in writing them, and as frequently burning what he had written after he had read them to me: many of them, which pleased me, I struggled to preserve, but without effect; for, pretending he would alter them, he got them from me, and thrust them into the fire." That he wrote the Odes to gain a present subsistence is but the tradesman's mistaken comment.

Gray was about four years older than Collins, and he survived him twelve years; he appears to have spent these years in gloominess and spleen; but we know not what intense pleasures he received from his solitary studies, from the improvement of his mind, from that exquisite taste and increasing erudition of which every day added to the stores. The enthusiasm of Collins was more active and adventurous, and his erudition probably more acute. Timidity and fastidiousness were great defects in Gray; they kept down his invention, and made him resort to the wealth of others, when he could better have relied upon himself. But as to borrowing expressions and simple materials, no genius ever did otherwise; it is the new and happy combination in which lies the invention. It may be doubted which are now most popular, the Odes of Collins or of Gray. On the one hand, what is most abstract is least calculated for the general reader; on the other hand, the variety of learned allusions in Gray renders the style and thoughts of his most celebrated Odes less simple, less direct, and less easily comprehended at once; but then his deep morality, the touching strokes which go immediately to the heart, his sensibility to the common sorrows of human life, his powerful reflection of the sentiments which "come home to every one's business and bosom," form an attraction which perhaps turns the scale in his favour. Of both these sublime poets the correctness of composition renders the writings a national good.

The French Revolution, which affected and partly reversed the minds of all Europe, produced a new era in our literature. There was good as well as evil in the new force thus infused into the human intellect. Our poetry had generally become tame and trite; a sort of languid mechanism had brought it into contempt; it was very little read, and still less esteemed. This might be not merely the effect, but also the cause of a deficiency of striking genius in the candidates for the laurel. Collins and Gray were dead; Mason had hung up the lyre; and Thomas Warton was then thought too laboured and quaint; Hayley had succeeded beyond expectation by a return to moral and didactic poetry at a moment when the public was satiated by vile imitations of lyrical and descriptive composition; but Cowper gave a new impulse to the curiosity of poetical readers, by a natural train of thought and the unlaboured effusions of genuine feeling. There is no doubt that a fearful regard to models stifles all force and preeminent merit. The burst of the French Revolution set the faculties of all young persons free. It was dangerous to secondary talents, and only led them into extravagances and absurdities. To Wordsworth, Southey, Scott, it was the removal of a weight, which would have hid the fire of their genius. But the exuberance of their inexhaustible minds in no degree lessens the value of the more reserved models of excellence of a tamer age. The contrast of their varied attractions supplies the reader with opposite kinds of merit, which delight and improve the more by this very opposition.

Authors seldom estimate each other rightly in their lifetimes. The race of poets, of whom the last died with the century, had little friendship, or even acquaintance among themselves; or rather, they broke into little sets of two and three, which narrowed their opinions and their hearts; Gray and Mason, Johnson and the two Wartons, Cowper and Hayley, Darwin and Miss Seward; but Shenstone, Beattie, Akenside, Burns, Mrs. Carter, Mrs. Smith, &c. stood alone. This is not desirable. Innumerable advantages spring from frank and generous communication. Collins and Gray had not the most remote personal knowledge of each other. Gray never mentions Dr. Sneyd Davies, a poet and an Etonian, nearly contemporary; nor Nicholas Hardinge, a scholar and a poet also. Mundy, the author of Needwood Forest, passed a long life in the country, totally removed from poets and literati, except the small coterie of Miss Seward, at Litchfield. The lives of poets would be the most amusing of all biography, if the materials were less scanty: it is strange that so few of them have left any ample records of themselves; of many not even a letter or fragment of memorials is preserved. None of Cowley's letters, a mode of composition in which he is said to have eminently excelled, have come down to us. Of Prior, Tickell, Thomson, Young, Dyer, Akenside, the Wartons, there are few of any importance known to be in existence. Those of Hayley, which Dr. J. Johnson has brought forward, are not of the interest which might have been expected. Mrs. Carter's are excellent, and many of Beattie's amusing and amiable: it had been well for Miss Seward if most of hers had been consigned to the flames. Those of Charlotte Smith it has not been thought prudent to give to the public. The greater part of those of Lord Byron, which Moore has hitherto put forth, had better have been spared: they are written in false taste, and are under a factitious character: in general, the prose style of poets is admirable; it was not Lord Byron's excellence. We have no specimens of the prose of Collins: it is grievous that he did not execute his project of The History of the Revival of Literature, or of the Lives for the Biographia Britannica, which he undertook. Poets of research are, of all authors, best qualified to write biography with sagacity and eloquence; they see into the human heart, and detect its most secret movements; and if there be a class of literature more amusing and more instructive than another, it is well written biography.

We have a few poets who have not possessed erudition; for genius will overcome all deficiencies of art and labour, such as Shakespeare, Chatterton, Burns, and Bloomfield: but it cannot be questioned that erudition is a mighty aid. Milton could never have been what he was without profound and laborious erudition. Another necessary knowledge is the knowledge of the human heart, which no industry and learning will give. It is an intuitive gift, which mainly depends on an acute and correct imagination, and a sympathetic sensibility of the human passions. Among the innumerable rich endowments of Shakespeare this was the first; it was the predominant brilliance of his knowledge which gave him correctness of description, sentiment, and observation, and clearness, force, and eloquence of language.

Collins had only reached the age of twenty-six when his Odes were published: what inconceivable power would the maturity of age have given him? It is lamentable that he had no familiar friend and companion from that period capable of apprehending and remembering his conversations. In his lucid intervals he must have said many wise, many learned, and many brilliant things; perhaps his very disease, in its vacillation between light and darkness, may have struck out many unexpected and surprising beauties, which common attendants were utterly incapable of appreciating. The flushes of the mind under the unnatural impulses of malady are sometimes inimitably splendid. His reason, at times, was sound, for his reason was fervid to the last. But it is said that his shrieks sometimes resounded through the cathedral cloisters of Chichester till the horror of those who heard him was insupportable.

All these speculations may appear tedious to those whose curiosity is confined to facts: but new facts regarding Collins are not to be had: and what are facts unless they are accompanied by reflections, conclusions, and sentiments? The use of facts is to teach us to think, to judge, and to feel: and facts, regarding men of genius, are valuable in enabling us to contemplate how far the gifts of high intellect contribute to our happiness, or afford guides for the rest of mankind; in what respects they have the possessors upon an equality with the herd of the people; and where they expose them to temptations from which others are free. For these purposes the ill fated Collins is a melancholy illustration: the Muse had touched the lips of his infancy, and infused her spirit into him; she had given him a piercing understanding, and an amiable disposition and temper; she enabled him to come forth with poetry of the first class, in the earliest bloom of youth; and to deserve, if not to win, the envied laurel, which millions have reached at in vain! What seeming glories and blessings were these! Yet to how few was so much misery dispensed as to this once envied being! May we not hope that his spirit now has its mighty reward?

Let it not be denied that there is high virtue in the culture of the mind, when directed to pure and elevated objects, and accustoming itself to travel in lofty paths! The mind cannot attain the necessary refinement, nor have its sight cleared of the film of earthly grossness, unless the heart throws off the dregs of coarser feeling, and keeps its wings afloat on a lighter and airier atmosphere. It may be said, that there have been bad men who have been great poets: but this position remains to be proved. The dissolute men who have written verses have not been great poets. Were Dante, Petrarch, Tasso, Spenser, Shakespeare, Dryden, Pope, Thomson, Burns, bad men? We know that Milton's character was great and holy, whatever were his politics: and who could be more virtuous than Gray, Beattie, Cowper, and Kirke White? And have we not virtuous poets among the living, men whose native splendour and intellectual culture have almost purified them into spirits? Let us never cease to meditate on the dejected inspiration, which could pour forth such strains as these:

"With eyes upraised, as one inspired,
Pale Melancholy sat retired;
And from her wild sequester'd seat,
In notes by distance made more sweet,
Pour'd through the mellow horn her pensive soul:
And, dashing soft from rocks around,
Bubbling runnels join'd the sound;
Through glades and glooms the mingled measures stole,
Or o'er some haunted stream with fond delay
Round a holy calm diffusing,
Love of peace and lonely musing,
In hollow murmurs died away."

There are those who will think the praises thus bestowed upon Collins extravagant. It is now sixty years since I became familiar with him; and I still think of him with unabated admiration. When the calm judgment of age confirms the passion of youth and boyhood, we cannot be much mistaken in the merit we ascribe to him who is the object of it.

S. E. B.

www.ingramcontent.com/pod-product-compliance
Lightning Source LLC
Chambersburg PA
CBHW061516040426
42450CB00008B/1647